KAJEEMAH

FEMALE CIRCUMCISION—MY TRUE STORY

(Including my Journey in Coming to America)

ELIZABETH YABA

Host of YABA TV

Tri-Star Publishing House
Long Beach, California 90805
424-789-9153
Email:yabatv@yahoo.com
www.yabamedia.com

Packaging/Consulting
Professional Publishing House, LLC
1425 W. Manchester Avenue Ste. B
Los Angeles, California 90047
323-750-3592
Email: Professionalpublishinghouse@yahoo.com
Website: Professionalpublishinghouse.com

Cover design: Emmanuel Fabiyi
First printing October 2017
ISBN: 978-0-692-96290-9
10987654321

Dedication

❧

Dedicated to me, Elizabeth Yaba, for being courageous to tell my "sawah sweet" story. It is my hope that others will use my example and hold on to God's Promises that never FAILS!

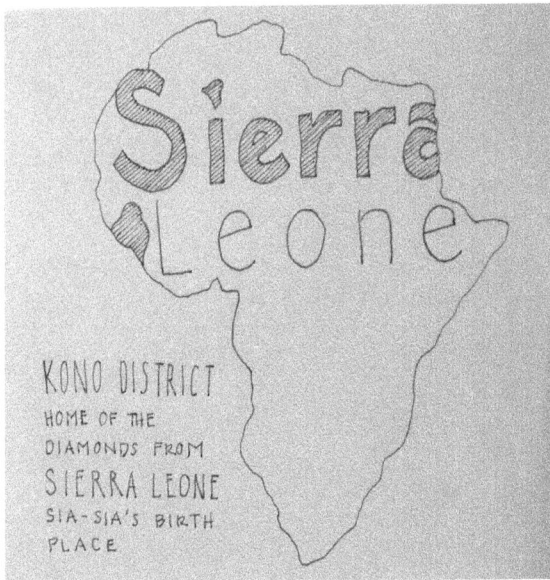

Sierra Leone

KONO DISTRICT
HOME OF THE
DIAMONDS FROM
SIERRA LEONE
SIA-SIA'S BIRTH
PLACE

Acknowledgements

❦

I would like to thank God for His directions to allow me to open up to write this book and tell my journey of life from Africa to America. Amazingly, it is important to know that God uses real people to take you to your destiny.

I am thankful for my Church, Springs of Hope Christian Ministries, and the Praying Pastors, led by Rev. Dr. Lawrence Lasisi.

I am also thankful to my friends and sisters in Christ Sade Olatubosun, and Dolapo Akerele Cole for their special loving support. In addition, I am also

5

thankful to Engineer Emmanuel Fabiyi for editorial and graphic work.

Special thanks go to James Meredith and his family for sponsoring me to the United States of America, and for teaching me, first-hand, the American Lifestyle. I remain forever appreciative.

Most importantly, I thank my two beautiful lovely daughters Sarah and Nanfo Downs for editorial work and design. Nanfo did the sketches. Finally, I am thankful to my dear brother John Yaba as well for all his moral support.

CONTENTS

FOREWORD

I honor and admire Elizabeth for sharing her story. This Book, Kajeemah, encompasses so much strength and power through her experience that can help normalize other women who experience shame, guilt, or embarrassment from under-going a similar journey. It takes much courage to take your broken pieces and make peace, and in return share that journey with the world as Elizabeth did. I believe women of all races, creeds, and journeys will be empowered by Elizabeth's boldness to be vulnerable in such ways as this Book describes. I hope that young girls across the globe obtain the privilege of reading this Book and it provides them with guidance and confidence to tell their story as well.

--

Dr. Bryant Youtube channels:

https://www.youtube.com/channel/UC8n1CvjdaIRpJPF8SZK3lmg

Thank you! Enjoy your day!

Dr. Bryant Team

http://www.drbryant.co

Dr. Cheyenne Bryant

NAACP President, San Pedro/Wilmington.

INTRODUCTION

I have been living as a modern day slave in my closet for over 30 years, right in the heart of Long Beach in Southern California, although the First Amendment says the opposite. Thankfully, I became liberated in my mind when I took the bold step and the courage to tell my story and also be the voice for the voiceless victims so that I can abolish the torture of fine young girls in Africa through female circumcision. In the village I was born in, Kono, Sierra Leone, the culture is strict and teenage girls go through many cultural odds. While some are to teach the girl the roles of womanhood, many of those cultures and traditions are nothing but unnecessary *pain*, such as female circumcision. The Elders of the village, with the approval of the concerned family, plan the ceremony which to them means preparing the teenage girl for womanhood and marriage. They believe that by circumcising girls, they would not be sexually active and be able to keep only to her husband. Even if he ends up marrying another wife, competition would not be a factor; why? Because, absence of the clitoris, they mistakenly believe the woman would be more sexually insensitive and thus, easily accept the husband's philandering with other women. When such ceremony is performed, they keep the girl for about 3 months in the bush until she is healed up completely and they feel she is ready to get married. I call this *modern day slavery*. Family traditions, morals, and the society in general almost dictates the happiness of young teenage girls, and it's nothing compared to anywhere else! My goal is to educate, and ignite self-esteem to the victims, while advocating to completely get rid of such gruesome act in parts of Africa where practiced, beginning with my country, Sierra Leone, so that girls can be as natural as nature intended them to be. This is a fight of a woman, but adequate education can help stop this non-sense. Would you join me in this fight to allow a young teenage girl to say NO to female circumcision and stand firm to live as natural as she was born - with a clitoris. You can help by buying this book and some of the proceeds will go towards this education. My coming to America is not only a positive life changing effect; it is also an excellent opportunity to end female circumcision. It reminded me of James H. Meredith, the first black man who attended a non-black school, the University of Mississippi with the protection of U.S. Marshalls, but he sets the record as the first Black Pioneer in the History Book. Why do I mention James H. Meredith here? I met him in Nigeria while I was visiting and he was on a short visit as well, and the driver assigned to take him around town on his tour lived in the same compound with me and he introduced me to Mr. Meredith. While almost everyone on his tour group was way too serious, like military personnel, I broke the ice by singing a song and he loved my bubbly personality on the spot. Then I heard him ask me … "would you like to visit us in the U.S.?" Really, although I heard him loud and clear, I thought it would be the biggest dream come true, so I was mute for a moment. 'Are you kidding me?' Then I exclaimed, 'AMERICA eh?' Even when those kind words from Mr. Meredith became a reality and I finally landed in the U.S in Cincinnati, Ohio, I would never forget two things: the lights at the airport were so bright, compared to the village I came from that lobbies electricity for 3 hours and the rest of the time is black-out. His wife, Judy, prepared a feast and asked me to take a shower first, then come to the dinner table. I went into the restroom and stood there for almost an hour still day-dreaming whether it was a reality I am in America, and looking at the bathroom so clean, with gold-plated sink, and lots of hair and body products to use. Honestly, you could pinch me, I would not feel a thing. I was so unexperienced that I did not know how to turn on the faucet. Judy asked, "Are you ok?"

'Yes' I answered and then I started to figure out things until the water was on. Today, I host my own television and radio shows, *Yaba TV* and *Yaba Radio Shows*. The Meredith family played a role in that too. Back then, 3-year-old Jessica Meredith noticed how I was unable to give eye contact when they were talking to me and asked her mom why? That was my turning point. Today my fans and viewers of my television show enjoy my dialogue, my charisma, and my verbal communication styles of the Shows. I also produce greeting cards with variety of African vocabulary words, translated. It's a non-fiction sad story with a successful conclusion, but for me I personally call it from *rags to riches!*

My journey of life to AMERICA has been a major roller-coaster, but through it all, FAITH in GOD has restored me!

M O T H E R

h o o d

CHAPTER 1

My humble beginnings

P lease allow me to briefly tell you what *KAJEEMAH* means. It simply means my head is so full and I've got to tell it all before it bursts …

I was born in a village; one of the most remote part of Sierra Leone, called *Sukudu*… which translation means headquarters of all witch craft activities. Ha… my humble beginnings … where I fetched drinking water from a place called *Semi-ni-koh*, the slowest still water stream that fills up and gets dried up quickly because the whole village depends on that little pond

Elizabeth Yaba

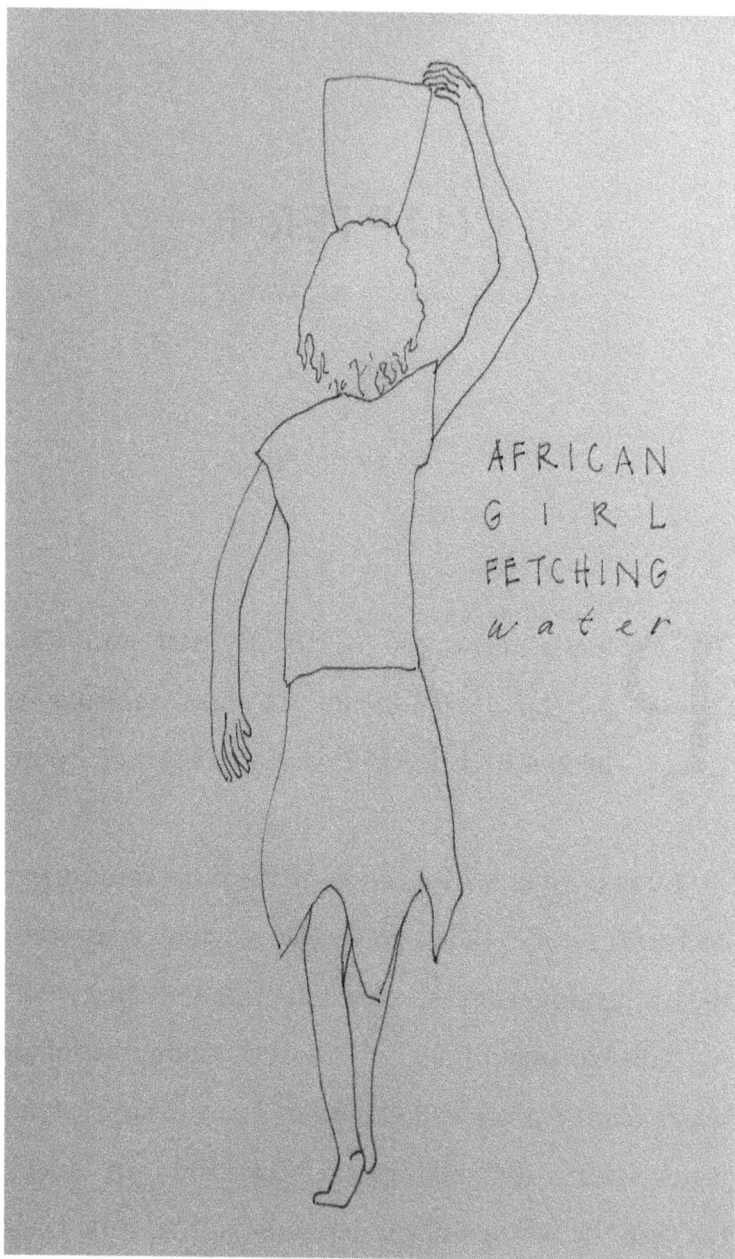

AFRICAN GIRL FETCHING water

18

as a source of drinking water. This water pond has frogs, fish, and some snakes. One can physically see them, but that was the only water source the village had for drinking.

Sia-Sia as mom Kumba Nanfo … called so early in the morning … We need drinking water, there is none. There I go. The busy scary road, the birds making noise, and the cock crowing that's all the noise I hear… I mumbled to myself.

I wish someone can come along to fetch water as well. I continued mumbling. I do not want to be the only one at Seminikoh.

Suddenly I heard someone call my name, Sia-Sia…

It's me Dara… as she had a bucket to fetch water as well.

Good morning … I spoke back to her.

Dara… what have you been up to Sia, I haven't seen you in a while

Sia-Sia… oh just busy with family and domestic work.

I am so happy to see you as well. I was mumbling to myself before you came along. I did not want to be alone at the river side at this early morning hours.

Dara... common Sia, its safe, why are you scared?

Sia-Sia, am not really scared but having a companion this early morning would make the work lighter. How is your family?

Dara answered ... everybody is fine.

Sia-Sia... you know Dara, have you ever thought about the water we drink from Seminikoh? Look at the frogs, the fish, the snake... they all live in that little pond we fetch our drinking water from, have you thought about how dirty the water may be and not safe for drinking.

Dara... ha... Sia, leave me alone. Our parents drank it during their time, and are still drinking it, so far, everybody is fine.

What side of the bed did you wake up today? Dara asked Sia-Sia...

hey Dara do you watch television? Have you seen American kitchen with running water from the faucet... Why don't we have it?

Dara... girl you said America, it's a super power country, why are you comparing our little country Sierra Leone to America?

Sia-Sia, but water is a basic necessity of life, why don't the leaders make available fresh, clean running water like every place else in the world? Why pond water?

Dara... leave that alone, this is what we have for now.

Sia-Sia... another thing is everyone uses their bucket to fetch the water, but realistically, some buckets are dirty. Some people have the same bucket for everything, that is; they bath from the same bucket, the only bucket they have; and also use for laundry, etc.

Dara ... Sia your mind is running too deep today, just calm down, we shall be alright. Our parents drank this same pond water so will be fine just like they are.

Sia-Sia...fetched the water and Dara too, back on the road going home with a bucket of water.

Mom Kumba Nanfo ... oh you are back? What took you so long today?

Sia-Sia… Dara, the girl next door came to fetch water too and we hang out a little bit.

Mom Kumba Nanfo …while she gives me instructions to clean up the living room, there is a lot going on in my head, that is the things I observe on a daily basis.

There was another running river called *Moinday*; however, it was extremely dirty and you can literally see and feel the dust. If you wash anything of white color, it instantly shows the un-wanted dark brown color patch you never intended to have on your pure white linen.

My family was so poor that we ate one-meal a day. Mama goes to the market and begs food from the *Muslims Jama*, jokingly asking … *Alaji mo pokite ofen-beh….* meaning what's in your pocket to give Alaji (aka Muslim prayer leader)? She would then buy dried bread that has been *unsold since 7 days*. Or buy mango, half rotten and we only ate the good side. When mom was able to buy a little grocery at any given time, she made sure that she taught me how to cook. Therefore, although she would not afford to give me lunch money or had any breakfast before going to school, she still waited for me to get back from school before she cooks. The part that I disliked the most - cutting onions, because tears run my eyes whenever I cut onions, that's the part she gave me to do. Her quest was

for me to learn how to cook with no reservation. She often told me that one day I would be somebody's wife and mother so there is no excuse for an African wife and mother who does not know how to cook. The situation was so rough for mom, so I started to do something about it. I wiggled to assemble crump of food items and ingredients from friends and schoolmates whose parents have businesses and produce which they sell at the general market. I would assemble as much as I can, then at midnight, I would manage to cook food on the charcoal stove behind the door. Though it's dangerous, open fire, I just wanted to feed my family. In the morning, neighbors would say that they smelled food last night, but I really didn't care much about it, I only care that my family did not go to sleep entirely hungry.

Sia-Sia … in the market

Fatu ….Sia, I have some left over rice and oil, would you like to have them?

Sia-Sia, sure, anything you can spare would be appreciated.

Fatu…here is a bag for you to put them so it's easy to carry. Also, if other friends have produce, you can fit all here…good luck girl

Sia-Sia … thanks … then I left. I went to Rugi.

Rugi…hello Sia, I thought you were coming over yesterday and I kept some dried fish and ogeri but I didn't see you. You may have them today if you like.

Sia-Sia…thanks a million, then I took them as well. I quickly left because it was getting dark and I had two more stops to make before going home.

Sia-Sia…with another friend… Nematu, how are you lady N, the nickname I gave her.

Nematu…fine she said. She continued I don't have much for you today but I have two ties of potato leaves and a bottle of red palm oil, so I took them and rushed out… thanks so much lady N.

Nematu…why are you rushing Sia?

Sia-Sia … most friends just called me for short Sia

I then told her that I needed to pick up something and I want to do it before it's too dark since I do not have a flash light.

Sia-Sia with Sebatu - my last stop. Sebatu is really generous. She gave me every thing else that were missing to make a complete meal.

Sebatu…Sia, take a little bit of everything that would enable you to cook your food completely.

Sia-Sia..girl, I can't thank you enough and I appreciate you all very much.

That's how I fed my family.

I had one slippers and it was the only one I used daily, which was used to go to school, to the market and every place I went. It was called "Bata" and also "Samah". When it tore down, I went to *Karankay*, that is remote shoe repairer. Thank goodness to "Mayi" that is the string from palm tree which was assembled and tired as the iron rope to strengthen my sandal I wear every day. At one time the sandal got so flat that I could feel the temperature of the soil when I walk.

Sia-Sia …hello Karankay…

Karankay …what do you need done this time?

Sia-Sia…my only slippers is loose and needs to be tighten so it can hold my feet…

Sia-Sia showing the slippers to Karankay.

Karankay…to be perfectly honest, your slippers needs to be replaced if you can afford to buy another one.

Sia-Sia …laugh

Life was not always like that. Before I was born, my father lived in England and worked as a Sea Man. My mother was a humble daughter of successful farmers from Yardu Sandoh. My grandpa was late Kondoh Gbemah Lebbie and my grandma was late Finda Nyaboi, a singer by profession too. She was a farmer and a singer. She and my grandpa had a plantation farm and they exported cocoa and kola nut. They were known in all the surrounding villages for their success.

As a result they were voted as the Village Chiefs and they were in charge of settling disputes in the surrounding villages. So when I was born, I grew up going on vacation to my grandparents where I acquired lots of wisdom. Life was much better with them. I learned a variety of African wisdom of handling and adjusting to any of life's situation, which gave me first-hand knowledge in my career today as host of YABA TV and subsequently Yaba Radio Show.

Some wisdom from my grannies

Grandpa ... *To-boi-me-bey-dia-asu-akoso-te-na-wah*

Meaning... a dance that would be great, you would know from the start.

This simply means a firm foundation of things last for a long time.

Grandma ... *to-boi-gba-adi-che-ma*

Meaning the best is yet to come.

That means do not settle for just anything because good things come to those who wait. It's worth it.

I was told my father married my mother at age 15 and she conceived me at that age. During that time, dad still had the financial strength and was able to maintain the family. I remembered wearing English Dresses from England dad brought for me and my siblings, I remember how the other villagers admired my English Dresses, I still remember how *Gbangah* Singers sang my dad's name praising the good things he has done, which drew out and flattened his wallet from money. Up till this day I look at their picture, that is... mom and dad, mom innocently looking like a 15 year old and dad looking like 45 years old. Can you imagine?

In America, it's considered child abuse, to claim this as (financial) protection of the young – though used as a maid - and convenient service for the old men.

Although my up-bringing was in a poverty environment, yet some family members were rich, but it's definitely not convenient to ask others for help even for a regular meal for the day. Here is how I spend a typical day:

1) Mop up the cemented kitchen floor with kerosene, even with that strong smell because

she could not afford to buy the regular cleaning products, but she was very neat.

2) Fetch drinking water from *Seminikoh*.

3) Long distance well-water fetch for laundry because *Moinday* river is extra dirty.

4) Go *poda-poda*. That is food search, survival for the fittest.

5) Yard to yard Mango search, that is go to neighbors that have fruits like mango, and pick them and bring for the family.

6) Go to the main market in search of Kongo Clothes, that is used clothing.

7) Walee-walee search… that is work for food at any rate.

8) Braid people's hair for a pocket change.

9) Help sweep people's compound for food or small change.

10) Fetch wood that would be used to cook the next opportune meal.

11) Help the *Maraka* tribe to beat *gara* aka tie-die cloth, for a fee.

12) Sell any excess fruits or items I got from hustling to help the family.

I was the FIRST born and my birth name is Sia. Then comes the second child, Kumba Theresa Yaba, then third child Shekuba Yaba, fourth child Kadiatu Yaba. Out of 12 birth from mom's first marriage, 4 of us survived then, but in 2010, one of my siblings died here in the U.S., Theresa Yaba. I sponsored and brought her to the United States. My mom's second marriage, she had three other children, Chesima, Bondu and Kamanda they are all still in Africa with the exception of John Yaba, whom I also sponsored and brought to the United States

My sister Theresa when she was alive . . .let's go window shopping

Sia-Sia … I like to go when I'm sure of some money in my purse.

Theresa…let's just go for the fun

31

Sia-Sia…you have never changed. Since back home you like to go adventurously.

Theresa . . .tell me the truth Sia, do you feel I am policing you when I call you many times asking where are you?

Sia… no. I know you care about me.

Theresa…that's because I want us to have dinner together, since you are gone all day and when you come home late you are tired

Sia-Sia…it's all good. So it came to me as a bomb shell shattered when the doctor told me that my sister will not make it from an illness. What choked me was, my mom died three months earlier, and my sister Theresa and I, along with some family members were planning a memorial service for mom, then Theresa got sick and for the doctor to tell me that she would not make it? I could not believe my ears. The Doctors at Harbor-UCLA Medical Center were very helpful and compassionate. I remembered even when I had faced the most difficult decision to sign a consent and authorization form for a surgery the doctors recommended for her before she lost speech, I was literally trembling, and worried "what if she does not make it?" They placed Theresa at ICU after the surgery and on life support machine. During the night when she does seem to cope well with the life support machine, they would call me to come see her and say good bye for the last time.

Ring ring…hello…this is the doctor from Harbor, we need you to come in

Sia-Sia… Oh my. Is she ok? But the doctor didn't sound positive. It was about 3 am, I then jumped in my car with my family, Nanfo, Sarah, John, all took off to the hospital. We stayed there for a couple of hours and when everything seem to be normal, we went back home.

We did that a few times, but unfortunately Theresa passed away on March 11, 2010 at 6 am that was when our world had never been the same. We lost dear Kumba. Although mom died three months before my sister died, I sobbed this time more than ever before. A sibling that was close, caring, and jovial; the absence was a big void within. It was harder for the folks back home since we buried her at in the U.S. at Cypress Forest Lawn. We still miss her till this day.

Sia-Sia . . .for a moment the village I was born Sukudu being translated headquarters of witch craft activities, I began to question would that have anything to do with the death of my mother Kumba Nanfo and the death of my lovely sister Kumba Theresa Yaba, three months apart?

Sia-Sia… I continued to deliberate for a long time, until one Sunday after church service, I felt the love of God in a special way that brought tears of appreciation that at least in all these I am capable to bury them respectively and on the healthy side. I was reminded of Psalm 30 vs. 5 that weeping may endure for a night, but joy comes in the morning. I did not acknowledge that scripture for a long time, because I was sobbing the death my loved ones, but thankfully today I feel the burden is light and I know that God is still in control of all things.

Here are some sequences of events in my life:

- At age 15… I was circumcised. No anesthesia, no kind of numbness, and using a curved knife called "Taambah" specifically designed for the act. So they cut off my clitoris. The process is very gruesome. The woman who cuts it is called Soko. The *Sanday Musu*, meaning the girl being circumcised, lay flat on her back with legs wide open. Then five strong women on each side hold her leg open until the act is done. When the clitoris is cut off, it's very painful and bloody. So they tie a rope on the waist line and cleave a thick linen fabric as pad, to uphold the bleeding, since a regular pad won't do. Then they applied a mint tooth paste, the same toothpaste people use to brush their teeth as medicine. Imagine mint on a fresh wound how painful it would be. When one urinate it burns, and during bowel movement, the wound expands so it doubly painful. When one cleans up with tissue it's sore and when water is used

to wash it, it's aggravatingly painful. The odor
is foul and there is nothing one can do to avoid
it. One lives with it for about three months
before a complete healing. I must not forget
to mention that it is a taboo to tell the story to
anyone not circumcised. And during the cutting
of the clitoris one is not supposed to cry or
scream to protect the family name. The family
is called a coward if the girl cries. I battled with
that for years even when I came to the United
States of America, and that is why I called this
book *Kajeemah*.

My faith in God stands out here when the song I
used to sing at the *Bondo* - Bush -comes to mind....
which says:

Jesus never fails' Jesus never fails; the man of the
world would let you down but Jesus never fails. . . Jesus
never fails, the man of the world would let you down
but Jesus never fails . . . Your mama would let you
down, your papa would let you down, your uncle will
let you down but Jesus never fails. REPEAT

Preparation of *Bondo* Girl starts three months before the actual date of the circumcision. At the initial stage, the family comes together, buy the *Bondo* Girl brand new outfits and make the announcement official. They put white powder made out of white rice and patch it on her face, then put "Kooh" that is Elephant teeth with a string through it and around the *Bondo* Girl's neck which symbolizes that it is official. The *Bondo* Girl is supposed to look like that every day for the three months duration until the final day when the entire ceremony is completed. After the circumcision, she can then dress normal. When she takes a bath and washes her face, she applies a brand new rice powder so her face continues to distinctly show her as *Bondo* Girl and in the process of circumcision.

Although some studies shows that female circumcision practice came from Egypt, Sudan, some Eastern part of Africa, it is widely spread across Africa and many people have done it and some are still practicing it; but, thankfully, Sierra Leone has somewhat stopped this gruesome activity. My goal is to see it stop completely, so girls can be as natural as possible.

Let me take you to the day of the circumcision. Early in the morning the family cooks lots of food to feed the crowd, and the dancers for the *Bondo* Girl. Then in the evening the dance becomes precedent and bigger. That is the transition between then and the now *Bondo* Girl, just hours away to be circumcised. The family hires traditional *Kono* singers and they perform to their best, while the general public dash and spray money on the *Bondo* Girl, called "Yongweh". For the rest of the evening she would keep getting money and someone keeps them all for her. Then, when the circumcision is done, with all the pain, she must be dressed up and she goes door to door dancing with more money sprayed on her, for now she's called a full woman ready for marriage in three months... how cruel, with all the pain, still must dance to show bravery, woah! Cold world eh?

Something weird happened to me and it was very unbearable. Two weeks after my circumcision, the *Soko* in her rounds of checking to see that the clitoris is indeed cut off, she claimed that mine was not done right and she made a big deal of it and got the family involved in a big way. Little did I know that they were about to cut me again. When the news was told to me I screamed. There was nothing I could do to avoid it. I was already in their hands, in the *Bondo* Bush recovering from the initial cut that was still very sour and tender. And because I screamed aggressively "What?" they maximized their strength with more women, "leg bearers" and cut me again. That was the 2nd circumcision I experienced. Let me describe the pain:

Pure lamentation, no frank appetite, only was thirsty for water, but the more water I drank, the more I had to urinate and that's more soreness. I hated food, knowing fairly well when I eat, I would need to pass stool and that had more pain because it stretches, extra sore, and strikingly painful. I disliked everything and every voice of so called courage for strength for womanhood. I was calculating in my head when I would have the opportunity to tell my story and free my mind, and that's why I called my story "Kajeemah", meaning tell it, and my head is so full that it could burst. That is from the Kono tribe.

When Life Gives You Lemons, Make The Sweetest Lemonade. I adjusted and found coping mechanism.

There is a saying that "you cannot cry over spilled milk" but you can surely do something about it not to spilled, and even when spilled, you can clean the mess.

Tips for the circumcised women

- Female circumcision is a gruesome act that so many young girls die from, but if one is lucky to be alive, then, there is definitely a need to celebrate and also share your experience with others. What is done cannot be undone in its 100% natural status even with modern day surgery in the United States, but one has to develop coping mechanism. Here are some:

  - Be friendly to your spouse or significant other in a more sincere way. This ability would allow you not to feel sorry for yourself but keep the romantic fire blazing and exciting. Personally, I do not like sad stories or feeling down, I keep things on the up-beat scale in every area of life; that is both business and personal. This ability seals my confidence as 100% woman with high class.

- When you are excited about the relationship, you also ignite fire in the other person and they are curious to feel the difference; but when you are sad and are feeling sorry for yourself, it puts weight on the relationship negatively.

- Develop the attitude that you are as good in bed and do not be shy about it.

- Be a communicator. Ask romantic questions in a friendly tone of voice. Then start hinting the other person softly. Start with … Have you ever heard about female circumcision in Africa? Then wait for the response and softly dissolve the conversation for another day.

- Do not be in a rush to jump in bed. Build a stronger romantic relationship and the real life's scenario relationship with your spouse first before you tell him the whole truth. You are not hiding things, but do not be in a haste to tell him things when your wings of love is not properly strong with him.

- This is where the American lifestyle really works, that is the First Amendment. Look straight in his eyes and express yourself.

- Make sure you have your favorite food or drink during that time, feed him a little to taste his feelings, that is if he is disappointed, hurt or feel sad.

- It is your responsibility to bring back joy if indeed joy is shaken because of the discussion.

- It is very important that you are not shy with your spouse or significant other and that you are open with your communication to build confidence in your relationship. Allow body language to work in your relationship.

- There would be no need to be jealous once your confidence level is high and this would allow you to have a happy healthier relationship.

- When life gives you lemons, you definitely can make not just lemonade, but make it very sweet. Strong odor is no long a factor with you, however; you can make it smell even more beautiful by creating your own "mixed solution of bath gel" to make it more appealing to your spouse. For example, at its worse, it smells like Onions. So you have a choice to smell like "Strawberry" every day. Yes, it's so easy for you to do that, so do it and make your world a charming place.

- For the men, do not jump into quick conclusion that the sexual appetite would not be the same. Have an open mind and also discuss your concerns with your spouse, but try not to nag about it. You may be surprised that your woman could be a lioness on bed. Two open-mindedness with tender care would make your loving world the most wonderful place to be.

- During child bearing, allow your spouse to play a key role in everything the doctor would allow him to do so that the bond carries over to the child. Do not hold on to the cultural mentality that you don't want the spouse in the delivery room. It's your life, make it very exciting, not just exciting!

Tips for the un-circumcised ladies

- When school is out, avoid going to spend time in the villages with your folks because they seem to be holding on that stupid circumcision ideology. This was one stronger reason I did not take my two girls to visit my home in Sierra Leone, Kono Land, so that some fanatic would not kidnap them and circumcise them.

- Spend time in the city where the law would cover you, that is, no one would force you to be circumcised, no, not in the cities.

- Protect your God given sex organ very tight because life will not be the same if you loose it, but you can only find your coping mechanism as I have mentioned previously.

- Bubble your berries and vanilla flavor even more and allow the sweet blend of nature to take its cause as you indulge yourself in them to give your body the greatest pleasure of smell. Enjoy, enjoy, enjoy!

- Above all, there is nothing that beats nature. So do your best and be as natural as you were born to enjoy your maximum potentials with your mate.

- At age 17 ... my biological dad put me in a locked room and whipped me literally with a branch of a tree, stripped off from the leaves and whipped me for complete 30 minutes, because he said I went on a date and I was too young, although it wasn't even true. I was discussing school works on literature

"MacBeth" but someone went to my dad and told him a lie and he did not investigate but only decided to whip me. My mother broke the door and got me out. That beating was so severe that I bled all over my body with cuts and bruises. I was unable to seat, stand, or lay down. It was so painful as though, one has fresh bruises, then salt and alcohol are applied as remedy. Imagine the pain. That was the reason my mom left him and forced her way to marry another man with already several wives and children, who mocked my mom to the fullest. His name was Kpakama, he is late as well. I grew up watching mom being cursed out by other women whom the 2nd husband had. Family chaos was all I saw when I was growing up.

Mongueh wife of Kpakama…. What are you doing here anyway? This man has three wives, why do you think we need you as the fourth wife? She asked my mom

Mom…as far as I am concerned, I am his wife just like any of you. We can make this either peaceful by accepting each other or the other way which would make all of us miserable.

Sia-Sia…my goodness I have never seen selfish set of people like my step dad's family. Everyone was not nice to me, my mother or my siblings. What did mom get into? This seems to be "from the frying pot to the fire"

Sia-Sia … opens up to mom…I don't think this marriage would work either because none of them like us.

Mom….be patient, they are not used to us, but with time, they will.

Sia-Sia…but honestly, I don't like them either. We are always fighting on petty little things such as who gets to drink from the only cup we all drink from.

Mom … it will be alright, just be a little patient…

- At that same age 17, while spending some time with my aunt Esther and her husband

Kaingbanjah, he got upset with me for domestic cleaning matters for no just cause and beat me up and ended up pulling my hair out…yes, my hair was all braided up in ponytail, and he ended up holding the ponytail and pulled it very hard and all my hair came out looking like a branch of a tree on one stalk.. I had no hair for a good 6 month. To my knowledge till this day, there was no law enforcement inquiry or punishment for his act.

- At that same 17 years old an extended family member, Yei Gbamanjah's son Aiah, looked at me right in the eye and cut me deeply with a sharp new razor blade on my right hand. While my hand is bleeding, Aiah laughed at his deeds. Up till today I have the scar. There was no justice for me in that matter as well. He had no reason for doing that but apparently just being wicked and there was no punishment by the law enforcement either for his act. So one is pretty much on your own …. "though luck".

- At the same age 17 I flew to Monrovia, Liberia, West Africa, in pursuit of happiness, but I did not find much luck in the country in my plight to come to America. Soon I returned home to Kono, Sierra Leone.

My brief moment in Liberia…

Sia-Sia… nice city Monrovia but I can't understand their accent although we are all Africans.

VILLAGE Dancers

Reuben …. Hi you girl…said Reuben, a Liberian… where are you coming from?

Sia-Sia…he tries a hold a conversation but I was not understanding some words so I left.

Sia-Sia… I managed to get a job in Monrovia at a furniture store "LPA Store" People rent furniture and pay monthly directly from their pay roll. It was a fun job, but I had to leave because I was searching for bigger opportunities such as coming to America.

- About 18 years old, I moved to Lagos, Nigeria. It was in Nigerian I got the opportunity to come to the United States of America.

Sia-Sia… woah, I've never seen a black population this big…yes, Nigeria is very big and predominantly Black. Technology is growing, and more commonplace than many African countries. At the time, Lagos was the Capital City and was very crowded. Almost every business person, especially foreigners, want to live in the Capital City. Life was fast-paced compared to the little naïve village I came from, or my brief moment in Liberia. Everything to me was fast-paced then.

Bunmi....Ekaro ma... Bunmi spoke to me... meaning good morning madam

Sia-Sia...yes ma, Ekaro ma... I had to learn to speak some Yoruba language since it was one of the main languages spoken in Lagos. But soon she discovered that I am not a Yoruba woman and not a Nigerian so she spoke Pidgin English to me.

Bunmi...for where you come from?

Sia-Sia...I am your neighbor, I abi Sa'Leone woman

Bunmi...with a big smile...so you know how to cook right? 'cause Sierra Leoneans are known to be good cooks.

Sia-Sia... with a smile nodding my head.

Bunmi....what are you doing in Nigeria? Who you come see?

Sia-Sia...my cousin is married to a Yoruba man, Denis Ola, they have four children, I just came to visit them.

Bunmi...you are welcome to Naija

Sia-Sia with a smile…thank you ma.

With all of these odds and growing pains, one still have to be very respectful. The definition of respect may be odd to Americans. In some West African Countries a child is not supposed to look straight into the eyes of an elderly person when talking to them and also not supposed to talk so elaborate to an adult. It is sign of disrespect. In my early teenage years, that's all I knew and practiced, but little did I know it's the opposite in the United States of America.

CHAPTER 2

My Turning Point

❧

Culture played a big role in my early years in Africa. When I came to America, life was very different. A 3-year old daughter of James and Judy Meredith, Jessica Meredith, taught me a lesson that I will forever remember…

"Mommy mommy she said with a BIG curious mind…why is it that when we talk to Elizabeth she is not able to look at us straight in the eyes to talk, but she looks at the floor and barely opens her month to talk? Says Jessica Meredith, a 3-year little girl.

Her mom, the wife of James Meredith, Judy Meredith, who was news anchor / journalist in Cincinnati, Ohio, then points out to me clearly that in the United States of America, {the First Amendment is that people express themselves boldly} and, culturally, they give eye contact to the other person they are speaking with; otherwise, it's considered disrespect or dishonesty. That was my turning point!

Prior to that, even when I was saying thanks to the Meredith family, I could not look into their eyes. There was nothing I did looking into any of their eyes. But who are the Meredith Family? Mr. James Meredith was the African-American who sponsored me to the United States of America. He was visiting Nigeria to introduce sanitation and queue to the Nation. I met Mr. Meredith through the driver that was assigned to drive him around town in his tours and that driver happened to live in the same compound with me, so he introduced me to Mr. Meredith. The first thing that Mr. Meredith said to me was … "You seem to be an intelligent young lady, you only need help, and we can help you. He continued ... I will be returning to the U.S. in two weeks, and upon my arrival home, I will send sponsorship documents for you to come to the United States to visit...would you like to visit us?" It sounded like a dream. Are you kidding me? All my struggling teenage life I had been looking for such a wonderful opportunity to come to the U.S. so I can revive my family to at least to afford a regular daily meal.

Amazingly, within two weeks I got all the necessary documents from Mr. Meredith and I left the soil of Africa for America. I came to Cincinnati, Ohio, where the Meredith family resided then. When I arrived at the airport, the Meredith family each had a placard saying welcome to AMERICA, ELIZABETH YABA. When they picked me up from the airport, Mrs. Judy Alsobrooks Meredith had a feast on the dinner table, and then she asked me to take a shower before I sat on the dinner table to eat. I was so excited to the extent I wasn't hungry although I had not eaten solid meal during the flight because I wasn't used to any of the food they served in the plane. She cooked macaroni and cheese, collard greens, beans, fried chicken, corn bread, hot dog etc., and when I looked at all the food, none was familiar to me as to the way I would cook it. Then she said try the hot dog, and I said ...."No I don't eat dog's meat" then she told me it's just the name but it wasn't dog's meat. I tried the collard greens, beans, mac and cheese and corn bread... and it was good. Up till this day, I still cook those food when I feel like eating American meal with the thought of the Meredith family.

Career-wise Judy was a major blessing. She took me along with her when she went to work as a newscaster. So I learned tips on television anchoring and programming through her the first time. It helped played a key-role in my success as a fluent host on both television and radio today.

A little about Yaba TV and Radio Shows:

Since my coming to America was engineered and sponsored by an African-American man James H. Meredith, and having lived here for even within the first two years, I noticed that there are some differences between the two, Africans and African-Americans; so, I developed a show to dialogue between the two based on first-hand-knowledge. What helped me to break that thick shell of low self-esteem was the wife of Mr. Meredith, Judy. Also Brooks Meredith, a journalist and anchor lady on Channel 5, in Cincinnati, Ohio, who took me to work in my early years in the United States, and showed me how it is done.

Judy….hey Sia-Sia you wanna go with me to the station?

Sia-Sia…yeah that would be great!

Judy…be quiet while we are in there because I would be announcing news, but keenly watch how it is done.

Sia-Sia…most definitely!

So the greater idea of Yaba TV Show did not only emerge from the Meredith Family admiration, but inspiration for talent and the energy as well.

Here is a typical show on Yaba TV or Radio

Topic: Cultural Differences

Guests: African, African-American, Indian and Mexican

First segment talks about each cultural background.

Second segment talks about the food differences and similarities.

Final segment talks about the social aspects of dating.

Then one closing remark from each guest...

One says patience, another tolerance, another love, and the last one adventurous.

After all these dialogue I bring fantastic music videos from two countries for entertainment sake, and I rotate to different countries every week. The Show airs on major station, Channel 13 KCOP, Saturdays at 11:30 AM. We are on a break now. My Show was rated the number one Sponsored Program on Channel 13 KCOP in 2015. And Yaba Radio Show airs on K-Day 93.5 FM on Sundays at 7:30AM, we are on a break as well. My slogan is. . . Make your weekend A Yaba Weekend!

CHAPTER 3

My America, the land of Milk and Honey

❦

The first five years of my life in America were truly a blessing to me and my family. My credit score was about 800, I had all kinds of major credit cards, cash, brand name cars, a house, career was beaming, and I travelled to many parts of Africa, meeting different African Presidents in their respective countries. I had my television show, I also had African clothing boutique and had a full-time job for 1-year that paid well. When Disneyland was expanding Mickey's Toontown, they gave the project to Skidmore, Owings & Merrill, a company which I worked for at the time, as a Word Processing Specialist. The company sent me on a training to be able to handle as a team player the specification typing of the project. It was a $2 Million project and we did it to completion. That was my last corporate job in America. Then I went into working for my own corporation full time, from that time till today, over 20 years. The one thing I must say though, I became shoe fanatic since I had only one shoe or sandal in Africa, but now I have over 50 pairs of shoe, all kinds of style, make and color.

Before branching off to work for Yaba TV, I sponsored two of my siblings from Africa to America. They both did very well in the U.S. but unfortunately one (Theresa Yaba) died in March of 2010 from cancer in the blood. My brother John is doing well still, although we all are still adjusting from our loss.

The beauty of my career here was fantastic and every country I visited, they had me on their National News which attracted the major businesses and the Chamber of Commerce to do business with me. Every country I visited, they had a Red Carpet Gala for my company and many "Who is Who" comes out to meet with me. I cannot express how rewarding those times were. Locally, when VIP's come in town, they would call me to cover their visit. Yaba TV grew to be a community house-hold name in South Los Angeles in particular while reaching the whole of Southern California.

The Show has interviewed so many high profile people in our community and in Africa. The Show became a point of conversation starter at many events.

CHAPTER 4

When all hell broke loose –
failed relationship, illness, business downturn,
loss of home, friends,
and I was left alone

❦

There is a saying that success attracts great people, but failure only does the opposite... But it's indeed true whom you choose as a spouse could make you or break you. Due to irreconcilable differences my relationship failed, then I got sick from the pressure, lost my house, then business failed, money got tight and friends were nowhere to be found! This is one part of any journey that the walking alone is no fun. One would feel as if you are day dreaming. Imagine I had everything, as described in Chapter 3, then waking up one day, it's gone just like that. These are the test of times to see who truly are your friends. Honestly, in my case, there were none. I asked myself over and over ... is that the real world...? Sadly indeed, it is. When it comes to bad news, it flies like a wild fire in the summer. Some people take pleasure in calling others just to gossip and each person tells his or her set of people and in a little time the whole community is circulated with the bad news.

The good news is ...I raised up above the circumstances, I re-established and the news started changing again. But please hear me loud and clear, I did not do it to please any person but for me, Elizabeth Yaba , Sia-Sia who always have a unique success drive that no one can take from me, no matter what the situation may be. My iron backbone came from Mr. James Meredith who said that ...the best of times come to an end and so do the worst of times, when one juggle the balance, life becomes easier for you.

ROUGH DIAMONDS

CHAPTER 5

The Unpolluted Lvoe of God never fails

❦

Throughout my ordeal I had to trust God to deliver me and show me the way, that is; His way that was destined from the time I was born. I had to exercise crazy faith, that is things that seemed so impossible, still believe to achieve them. The Bible said in Hebrews 13 verse 8… Jesus Christ is the same yesterday, today and forever; therefore, I stand on that His promises which were fulfilled in the Bible to also manifest in my life and to come shinning like gold …

1) Weeping may endure for the night but joy cometh in the morning… Psalm 30 vs. 5

2) David defeated Goliath because he trusted God to fight for him … 1 Sam 17 vs. 45-50

3) The Lord promised His Children Power to conquer ALL the power of the enemy Luke 10 vs. 19

4) The Lord has not given us the Spirit of fear, but of Power, Love and Sound Mind II Timothy 1 vs 7

5) He is the God that healeth, Jehovah Rapha … Psalm 103 vs 3

6) He is also the God of provision, Jehovah Jireh … Psalm 23

7) He knows everything about His Children as the Creator … Elohim … Psalm 139 vs 7-14

What all these scriptures have in common is that no matter how challenging any situation may be, if only you can look beyond your dark moments and focus on the true promises of God, He will bring you through at His own timing!

CONCLUSION

If this Book can disseminate this information among my readers, then I have done my due diligence and I would be the happiest Bondo Girl on earth … lol.

Above all, I am forever thankful for the amazing grace and LOVE of God for keeping me alive, yes! alive indeed!! and was able to get over all the odds and tell my story. I am thankful for the free Spirit of America, although it took me so long to speak out, but I finally did… bravo to the First Amendment. I sincerely hope you enjoyed reading this Book and do look forward to future Books!

About the Author

Elizabeth Yaba, aka Sia-Sia, host of Yaba TV and Radio Show, a contemporary African Show designed to bridge the cultural divide between Africans and African-Americans based on first-hand knowledge. In my opinion everyone needs to play a part to bridge that cultural divide. A typical Show dialogues with guests from diverse backgrounds that bring ideas, facts and realities to the table to allow understanding of the cultures of the very different panels. The Show, Yaba TV was established in December of 1992, 25 years ago. Some guests include: former Los Angeles County Supervisor Yvonne Braithwaite Burke, former Congresswoman Diane Watson, Councilman Bernard Parks, former President of Ghana Jerry Rawlings with special appearance by the late super star Michael Jackson at the Beverly Hilton Hotel in 1995 when the former President Jerry Rawlings visited Los Angeles. Other guests were singer Stevie Wonder, Isaac Hayes, and many more. On February 15, 2000 I was a guest on Black Entertainment (BET Tonight) with Tavis Smiley and Sheryl Martin. That interview was LIVE and NATIONWIDE and BET sponsored my trip to Washington and back to Los Angeles. On December 16, 1999 I was featured on the Los Angeles Sentinel on Section B-5, the article of which can be found at the Black Resource Library on El Segundo Blvd in Los Angeles. February 2015 I was featured on Good Day LA on FOX 11. Google …FOX TV / Yaba TV. You may find some of my Shows on Social Media; look for the Peach and Blue outfit and find all the celebrities mentioned above along with myself on YouTube: Yaba TV. May 1, 2015, I was a guest on 94.7 The Wave with Pat Prescott on Hollywood Report. Show aired on Channel 13 KCOP Saturdays at 11:30AM, also aired on KJLH Radio 102.3 FM Sun. at 6:30pm and K-Day 93.5 FM Sun. @ 7:30 am. 25 years of experience with some college, natural wisdom from the Motherland, real hands on work experience has given me fluent ability to appropriately manage the Shows.

Thanks a million and God Bless!!